PREPARE
TO BE
BOARDED

PREPARE TO BE BOARDED

A Coast Guard's Remarkable Life

LINDA HALEY PRENTICE

Copyright © 2024 Linda Haley Prentice
All rights reserved.

PREPARE *TO BE* BOARDED
A Coast Guard's Remarkable Life

ISBN 979-8-9916434-1-2 Paperback
     979-8-9916434-0-5 Hardcover
     979-8-9916434-2-9 Ebook

To Mark J. Prentice, Chief Warrant Officer (CWO3) U.S. Coast Guard Retired, the inspiration for this book. I am proud of your service to our country throughout the course of your career. Larger than life, always in motion, you make the most of every hour; no wonder you've accomplished so much. I love you.

CONTENTS

INTRODUCTION 1

CHAPTER 1: MARK J. PRENTICE,
              LIFE IN THE COAST GUARD 5

CHAPTER 2: MARK J. PRENTICE,
              LIFE AFTER THE COAST GUARD 51

CHAPTER 3: MARK J. PRENTICE,
              A NEW COAST 65

CHAPTER 4: MARK J. PRENTICE,
              SNAPSHOTS FROM THE COAST 81

ACKNOWLEDGMENTS 109

INTRODUCTION

FIRST, I WAS NEVER GOING TO REMARRY AFTER MY HUSBAND, Pat, died; second, the Coast Guard patrols the waterways—it was that simple. I believed both were true until I met Mark. Boy, was I wrong! He was about to change my life in every way, and I never saw it coming. So much for the absolutes of never.

After Pat died, I resolved to remain single. I did, however, go on a dating website thinking I would find friendship and perhaps someone to travel with. I wasn't looking for any more than that, and certainly not marriage. I knew I could never replace the kindest man I had ever known. Fourteen months later, I met Mark. I was very up-front with him and explained my (above-mentioned) plans. He smiled, nodded, and then informed me that he had been married for forty-one years when his wife died, and he had every intention of being married again.

Other than our relationship goals, we had everything else in common. We are both veterans—him of the Coast Guard, me of the Navy. We both have a strong background in volunteer work. We both cared for our spouses in their last years. We both love golf, and both of our mothers were born on November 5th! (How random is that?) It took no time at all for me to forget my resolve to stay single and fall for Mark—hook, line, and sinker. He was larger than life and made me over-the-top happy.

In order to know Mark, I had to know more about the Coast Guard. Surprisingly, for all my time in the Navy, I knew little of what the Coast Guard actually did and how they did it, so I began to learn more about it. I started to ask friends and family, "Did you know XYZ about the Coast Guard?" They didn't either. No one seemed to understand the purpose and workings of this branch of the military, especially outside of the water.

For many, everything they know about the Coast Guard may be based on the movie, *The Guardian*, with Kevin Costner and Ashton Kutcher—a flawed perspective. According to the Coast Guard Academy, the units have multiple missions as America's Maritime Guardians, saving lives and deterring complex threats—from disrupting transnational crime and terrorism, to preventing cyber threats to our ports, to addressing the impact of human activity in the polar-regions as ice caps recede.

Mark Prentice's Coast Guard experiences are the real deal. He and other "Coasties" are true heroes. They go out to sea in lethal weather—weather that helicopters won't even fly in. They have embraced the slogan, "We have to go out, but we don't have to come back." Their stories need telling, and I'm driven to write them down and get them into the hands of Coast Guard friends and family. I'm starting with the story of my favorite Coastie.

> **SIDE NOTE:** You wouldn't believe how many famous people are Coast Guard veterans. For example, Arnold Palmer, Jack Dempsey, Lloyd/Beau/Jeff Bridges, Cesar Romero, Victor Mature, Ida Lewis, Buddy Ebsen, Alex Haley, Michael Healy, and my own Publishing Consultant, Rose Friel's Grandfather, Captain Gordon Hempton—they're all "Coasties." Additionally, although he never served, it is worth mentioning that Walt Disney and his staff pledged their unfaltering support to the war effort during World War II, with the studio devoting over 90 percent of its wartime output to producing training, propaganda, entertainment, and public-service films, as well as publicity and print campaigns—all without any profit. In fact, Walt Disney is responsible for the logo used during World War II for the Coast Guard Corsair Fleet.

This book is an intimate look at the life and career of a "Coastie" (Mark)—the Coast Guard from one man's perspective—and the honor of him sharing it with me.

CHAPTER 1
MARK J. PRENTICE, LIFE IN THE COAST GUARD

"Semper Paratus is our guide, our pledge, our motto, too. We're 'always ready,' do or die! Aye! Coast Guard we fight for you!"
—Coast Guard Mantra

FAMILY AND MOTIVATION

Mark's father served in the Army during Vietnam. Mark lived a typical military kid life. They were stationed overseas in Germany and France, as well as many places in the United States, such as Virginia, Washington, and Colorado. Eventually, the family settled in Texas.

Early on, Mark experienced some of the horrors of military life. When he was five years old, two Army soldiers came to their front door. This type of visit usually meant the Army was there to inform you of bad news, such as the death of a family service member. At the time, Mark's father was deployed to Vietnam, and Mark and his mother were the only ones home. Mark's mother panicked. She refused to answer the door and instead called her father who came to the house right away. After speaking with the Army personnel standing outside, he realized that they had come to report a death, yes, but they were at the wrong house! Mark's father was not dead. He was alive! A regrettable mistake (with a silver lining) that left a lasting impression on a small child.

> On a lighter note, one day Mark's mother fell and broke her wrist (that is not the lighter note). She'd used a bar stool as a step stool to reach an object on an upper shelf. The bar stool shifted underneath her, and she fell, breaking her wrist. That Sunday, Mark went to church without her since she was not yet feeling up to going. When the priest asked Mark where she was, Mark replied, "She broke her wrist falling off a bar stool." When Mark told his mother, she gasped, "You did not tell the priest I fell off a bar stool!" He quipped, "I couldn't lie to a priest now, could I?"

Mark's father eventually came home from Vietnam. He had contracted hepatitis while overseas and recovered at Walter Reed

Hospital. He also sank into a deep depression. He had killed his share of people in Vietnam, and it tormented him. It was because of this that his father never wanted his sons in the military, specifically because they might have to kill people. He dove into drinking and became an alcoholic. He hung out at the American Legion and VFW hall. That was the only place in town to get alcohol in their dry county. Of course, drinking at home was an option, but he wanted to spend time with his Army buddies.

Max and Margie Prentice, Mark's parents.

Those were different times, and one day in 1968, after Mark's family uprooted to Fort Lewis, Washington State, Mark rode with his father to the base. Angry protesters met them at the gate shouting profanities and accusations ("Baby Killer!") while throwing rotten vegetables, garbage, and tomatoes (blood effect). Eight-year-old Mark hid in the back seat. People did not realize that while they were protesting the war, they were traumatizing the children of the veterans they assaulted. Mark was confused and frightened, and never lost his resentment of "hippy-type" protesting people. On a positive note, that experience made Mark a red, white, and blue, flag-waving American who loves his country.

When Mark was a few years older, his father bought him his first gun to shoot (a boy ought to know how to shoot), but he refused to take Mark hunting. That may sound ironic, but Mark's father never wanted to kill anything or anyone ever again, and he certainly didn't want his son to either.

Fast forward to 1978. Then seventeen years old, Mark Prentice knew he wanted to join the Coast Guard after seeing a television commercial during a Saturday Night Live episode with his friends. The commercial showed the Coast Guard on the Great Lakes, and Mark knew two things: (1) he wanted to get into law enforcement, and (2) he was infatuated with the water. This was the era of Jacques Cousteau after all, and the Coast Guard blended law enforcement with maritime life.

When Mark joined the Coast Guard, his father viewed it as redemption for the family legacy. His father embraced him every time he came home on leave, proud because his son did not take lives—he saved them. All the Army taught his dad was to "blow sh*t up and kill people," but the Coast Guard—they were in the business of saving people!

> Mark and the Coast Guard share the same birthday: August 4th. Wherever Mark was stationed, there was a celebration on August 4th, and Mark's name was usually added to the cake.

THE U.S. COAST GUARD

On August 4, 1790, the Coast Guard was established by Alexander Hamilton as the Revenue Marine Service (later the Revenue Cutter Services or RCS). When George Washington signed the Tariff Act that authorized the construction of ten vessels to enforce federal tariff and trade laws and prevent smuggling, the RCS was established under the U.S. Secretary of the Treasury Department. In 1915, the RCS combined forces with the U.S. Lifesaving Service (previously formed in 1878), and the Coast Guard was born. It is the nation's first afloat armed force.

There are more than ten times as many active-duty Army personnel as there are active-duty Coast Guard, and there are more people in the New York City Police Department alone than in the Coast Guard.

Because of their sheer numbers, members of the Navy, Army, Air Force, and Marine Corps have the luxury of specializing in individual career paths, which is what those branches need. That's not so with the Coast Guard. Because the Coast Guard is so much smaller than the other branches of the military, cross-training is mandatory. Everyone on a boat becomes proficient at multiple tasks and soon becomes invaluable. If something breaks on their boat, there's no putting in a work order or requisition—they find a way to fix it themselves. They have to! It's an agile, maneuverable structure for a military branch, and it attracts adventurous problem solvers.

Did you know that members of the Coast Guard are trained in Level A Chemical Response like the Environmental Protection Agency (EPA)? They work with Customs, Transportation, the FBI, the DEA, the military, local law enforcement (Mark, specifically, in Houston, Port Arthur, and Atlantic City), and as EMTs.

Mark excelled at cross-training in engineering, law enforcement (LE), navigation (ship handling, coxswain), emergency medical services (EMS), firefighting, hazardous materials, Sr. Marine Inspector (international maritime LE), and Command Enlisted Advisor. When I was in the Navy, we "specialized" in our jobs. When I was stationed in Gander, Newfoundland, the Canadians (like the Coast Guard) did not have the huge personnel that the U.S. Navy has, so they cross-trained their personnel just like the Coast Guard, with every able service member wearing many hats, so to speak.

I met my first Canadian counterpart when I was stationed in Hawaii, and I was so impressed at how many areas of communications he was proficient in (as I was a "specialist" in my one area). I was determined to go to Gander as my next duty station. At the time, Gander was a coveted position for ten Americans, and only E-5s and above were authorized to go. I was an E-4, but I worked my butt off, was nominated for Sailor of the Quarter, and secured the transfer with a note from the Chief, and the experience was everything I expected. Remarkable people just like Mark and the Coasties.

> Mark attended a Marine Firefighting and Emergency Training Course. The Marine Firefighting course was located at the Treasure Island Naval Base. Coming off the CG cutter, Mark and his shipmates looked pretty shabby. Their dungaree uniforms were freshly cleaned but grease-stained, and therefore, looked filthy. As a result, shore patrol picked them up and escorted them off the base. When they returned to the boat, they informed the Captain that they were kicked off because they were "unpresentable in uniform." The Captain laughed hard because the shore patrol did not realize where the men had come from. He ordered them back to the base, made the necessary phone call, and the men made it to class.

Being on a small cutter, a 110-footer, Mark was often on deck performing the humbler tasks that are generally associated with those of lower rank—but in the Coast Guard, everybody pitches in. For instance, carrying supplies to the boat, moving supplies, cleaning, basically anything Mark could do, he would do to help his crew; he was not afraid to get his hands dirty. This wasn't always the case with members of the other military branches of service. Consequently, at times, someone would mistake Mark for a Bosun Mate (short for Boatswain) rather than the Chief or Officer he was. It was usually a Lieutenant or Junior Officer from another branch of service who would yell, "Hey, Bosun!" An honest mistake based on the grunt work he was doing at the moment, but Mark would feign insult and offense. "That's Chief Engineer to you, jackass!" Yep, the work ethic aboard a Coast Guard ship was a bit more egalitarian, and Mark took those opportunities to highlight it.

Mark Prentice spent five years performing those duties, and overall he loved the Coast Guard, but for the record, he said, "It was a shi**y job." He regularly was exposed to poison ivy, and once he was even attacked by ground hornets when he felled a tree. Good times? Not!

DEVOTION

One of the first things Mark told me about the Coast Guard was that there could be hours of boredom followed by moments of sheer terror. Hearing the phone ring could trigger him because he never knew when disaster or family-disrupting urgency would take him away from home. The caller usually gave Mark a one-hour notice to report for duty. It was not a request; it was an order. Mark felt this firsthand while home on leave on more than one occasion. The phone would ring, and it was his Captain. One time he dropped the phone because he felt so completely emotionally drained. He had been out for duty for 266 days and had his heart set on recharging with his family. But, devoted to the Coast Guard, Mark picked the phone up off the floor and reported for duty. It was exhausting.

Once, he came home on leave and, when he pulled up to his house, the military van was already there waiting to take him right back to the boat. It can feel devastating to have your home leave snatched away at the last minute right when you were feeling the need for it the most. Mark said this "carries with you for the rest of your life." He does not use the term Post Traumatic Stress Disorder (PTSD) for any of his experiences; he puts on a brave front, but the symptoms, stress, and triggers are all real.

Life was stressful not only for Mark, but also for a military spouse and family, and the deployments (some scheduled but some by emergency) were even harder. Mark explained, "Every damn time I was scheduled to deploy, there would be a fight [with my spouse], and there was nothing I could do to stop it. The men feel obligated to go and feel guilty for leaving; the wives feel anger or fear over the coming separation and responsibilities as a single parent." It got to the point that the family hated when the phone rang. Mark's late wife, Susan, was a faithful wife but picked fights in the days leading up to deployment. I have heard the same dynamic from other military spouses as well. Deployments can bring out the good, the bad, and the ugly in couples.

I never met Susan, and she is not here to share her experience, but my friend Rana, a military wife, provided some insight into what may have been Susan's thoughts and experiences. For example, Rana would find herself avoiding her husband just before he was to be deployed. The combination of separation and loneliness—taking on the full responsibility of the children, bills, house, cars, etc.—could be overwhelming. Rana explained, "As a dependent, when your spouse is deployed, depending on how often you can communicate, the talks are about how everything is fine and all is good. You never talk about the bad—how the car broke down, the tears that were shed, etc. You learn to lean on a network of friends and have a list of numbers to call if you need help." Whether picking a fight or avoiding the spouse, both are coping mechanisms to prepare for the separation to come.

> Indulge me for a moment please, while I tell you my favorite Rana "deployment story"—a time when she was stopped by a police officer, and her disposition was definitely less stoic. The officer pulled her over because her car registration had expired. She would not have known that because her husband took care of the cars before he left for deployment, but he missed this one. It flustered Rana to get pulled over. On top of that, the officer (while writing the ticket) made the unforgivable mistake of asking her for her weight (it is not listed on a person's driver's license in Texas). That was too much to bear, and her exasperation gushed out, "My husband is deployed, I'm getting a ticket, and on top of all that, you want to know my weight?!" The officer sensed the urgency to de-escalate and mumbled something to the effect, "Ummm, 120 lbs" and let her go with a simple warning. I bet the officer thought twice before asking another woman her weight again.

Even when Mark wasn't deployed, military life could be challenging. One year just before making Chief, Mark and his wife were invited by the Captain to a Christmas party at the Captain's home. He was close to the Captain who was also an engineer—mutual respect all around. But, most of the people attending the party were officers or chiefs. Mark was the only E-6 attending.

He hesitated to accept the invitation because he and Susan had a three-year-old child at home, and getting a babysitter was not easy. The Captain said, "Bring the baby too!" *Well, ok,* Mark thought. They went and had a great time, and the Captain carried the baby around the party like a football trophy. All seemed well until afterward. One of the officer's wives (who was a friend of Susan's) told her that she caused a huge scandal with the other wives because it was an adult party, and they had the nerve to bring a baby! "They just didn't belong." Regardless of the contempt, Susan had friends on base and weathered it in support of her husband.

Mark was devoted to the Coast Guard, and his family's support helped him to serve our country admirably.

> *"[Mark] is hard working and a conscientious sailor. He is a good leader, and is the type of man who gets things done."*
> —Letter of Appreciation from the Coast Guard, 24 November 1980, regarding Mark's part in saving over 500 lives in a gasoline spill.

OUT AND IN...TROUBLE

Mark was honorably discharged from the Coast Guard in 1982. However, under contract, he was still in Inactive Reserve status. In 1984, the Coast Guard contacted him requesting that he reenlist to Active status. The Coast Guard needed good engineers, and Mark had a reputation for being the best. Under normal circumstances, a re-enlisting service member who's been out for two years would return to service at a reduced rank and go through boot camp for refresher training and new uniforms. Not Mark. Because of his skills, Mark was ordered directly to the boat at the full rank he'd previously attained, and his uniforms were sent ahead for him there. That's how urgently they needed his skills. He reported directly to Port Arthur, Texas and was assigned to the Marine Safety Office (MSO) as their pollution investigator and Hazard Inspector.

After Port Arthur, Mark transferred to the Arctic base at Port Clarence, Alaska for an isolated tour. Isolated tours are usually too inhospitable for service members to bring their family members with them. The service member transfers without them, and the family is left behind for a separation of six months to a year (or longer). One more harsh stressor on the family as Mark left them behind and traveled to Alaska. These orders came with a note, "Do not report in uniform as this is inadequate protection for extreme cold." Coming out of Texas, Mark was equipped with tropical uniforms and received his Arctic gear when he arrived.

> I never received a note like that when I was in the Navy. I transferred from Wahiawa, Hawaii to Gander, Newfoundland with no such note. I left Hawaii in the

standard military uniform of the day—short jacket, nylons, and two-inch heels. I stopped in Michigan for a visit, and my mother had the good sense to look ahead to where I was going. She bought me a gorgeous pink goose down parka for my stay there. I was completely ill-equipped for the weather ahead, and when I arrived in Gander, it was nearly twenty below. I was carrying that pink parka, and if that wasn't bad enough, the airline lost my luggage. While I was waiting for the van to pick me up to take me to the base, it didn't take but minutes before I was freezing and wondering what the hell I was doing standing in this weather wearing a summer uniform with nylons and heels! I put on that parka and hoped for the best for my feet while I waited for transportation. When I got to the base, I was confronted by a chief who noted I was out of uniform, and I had no problem informing him that the airline lost my luggage. He backed down when he saw my feet. Back to Mark.

It all began with Mark's first bush plane trip. This tiny plane barely held two people, and somehow this thing became airborne and fluttered over ice and snow with no human in sight below except a lonely dog sled team. Typically, bush planes transport mail and supplies to remote areas, not people. In flight, Bob the bush pilot wrote in his flight log while steering the plane with his eighty-eight-year-old knees. This unnerved safety inspector Mark. It was the smallest plane he had ever been on. Even cars have inspection stickers, and Mark searched the windshield for a meaningful sticker of the sort. *Is this thing even airworthy?* he thought, though his life was already entrusted to it. Distracted by his flight log, the pilot did not see the mountain filling the windshield indicating they were headed for certain disaster—like a scene from a cartoon. Mark motioned excitedly. The pilot glanced up, and nonchalantly veered to the left to circumvent it. Mark thought, *Does this pilot have a death wish, or does he know something I don't?* As far as a heart rate elevator, the flight had nothing over the landing.

The plane fought against strong winds toward the general area of the landing strip and somehow landed sideways in an adjacent parking lot. Mark was surprised to be alive, but Bob the bush pilot remained unphased. At this point, Mark believed being cast overboard in shark-infested waters in a raging sea storm seemed less frightening than this bucket of bolts hiccupping through the skies at the hands of its geriatric pilot. Or maybe, just maybe, one man's courage is for the sea, and another man's courage is for the skies.

This duty station was seventy-two miles from Russia, called the Big Diomede Islands. The U.S. is called the Little Diomede Island. Port Clarence was the duty station for Long Range Aids to Navigation (LORANSTA). This would be Mark's home for the next year. And the dozen Coasties he was serving with would be practically his only link to humanity. Back in the day, at this point, Mark would have experienced an "induction" (translate: hazing) to Port Clarence. Mark had been inducted before. He was made to wear thigh-high boots, the crew filled them with snow, and he was expected to walk and carry snow from one point to another. Painful but temporary, right? Wrong! Mark's legs fell to frostbite. Inductions are not just a Coast Guard thing—we had them in the Navy—but for my induction to the Canadian Forces Base (CFB), I was highjacked in the hallway and pummeled with shaving cream. No frostbite or bodily damage. Although it had never happened before (or after) with other service members, the experience left Mark with permanent nerve damage to his feet and legs that has lasted decades. Mark now wears a neurostimulator in his back for the constant pain.

Some things are better left in the past, and nowadays, hazing is illegal in the military—as it should be—so Mark did not have to endure another hazing this time around (unless you count the flight of terror).

> The first time Mark thought he might be some animal's lunch was a day they boarded a Japanese fishing ship that was in United States waters. Mark was boarding from a small,

twenty-five-foot engineer's boat, and a massive orca came alongside. That killer whale was bigger than their boat! Then it blew its hole too. Mark was only eighteen at the time, and it "scared the sh*t" out of him. Killer whales followed factory fishing boats for food. When the fish were caught and processed on board, orcas feasted on the waste thrown overboard. Mark was hoping not to be their next snack.

There were plenty of other terrors in the Arctic. Mark thought he might be food for wildlife when he and another shipmate were three-wheeling. Visibility was poor, and at twenty-five miles per hour, they drove up on what appeared to be an Eskimo in a big parka hovering over a whale carcass. Mark and his shipmate slammed on the brakes. At that moment, a huge grizzly reared up at them! That was no Eskimo in a parka, and it (again) "scared the sh*t out of them," and they backed away to a safer distance.

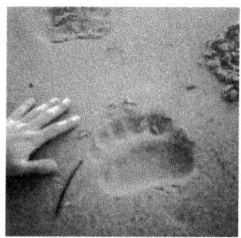

Mark's (silverback colored) grizzly paw print in the arctic.

It wasn't all scary. Mark was on base, and there was a storage shed on the compound from the old World War II days. There were six-foot cylinder helium tanks (for launching weather balloons) being stored in the shed—thousands of them just sitting in storage because they no longer launched weather balloons so close to Russia. *Let's avoid that international incident*, they thought. The shed also housed an old broken snow plow. When Mark and the crew were bored (and there may have been alcohol involved, but it cannot be confirmed or denied), Mark decided to fix the old snow plow. Let's just say that while fixing said snow plow, the crew had fun with the helium and talked like Daffy Duck for weeks.

One of the downsides of working in the Arctic was that everything was white. So it was regrettable when green or camouflage vehicles arrived. The colored vehicles made an easier target. The colors in the Arctic were either black or white, so throwing Army green into the environment made them stick out. Black and white camouflage would have made more sense, but they were given green vehicles.

Communications back then were over a Very High Frequency (VHF) Marine radio, and knowing they likely would be monitored by the Russians, the crew had fun with nicknames. The green truck was christened "Green Hornet" and the camouflage vehicle was "Rambo." Mark would radio in, "Rambo to Green Hornet." Arctic fun on the radio.

A certain 1,400-foot tower needed regular maintenance. Most sailors would climb to 700 feet—the point where you could no longer see the ground below—and then retreat back down the pole. Mark was one of the few sailors who made it all the way to the 1,400-foot top. Brave or "more balls than brains"? Let the reader decide.

The supply plane landed every two weeks to drop off necessary supplies. The pilot would help unload and go inside to socialize for a while before returning to base. One time the pilot flew in and saw the crew in their long underwear and mukluks—all of them! Not even a hint of an official uniform. That was the one time the pilot did not get off the plane; he got airborne as soon as possible. He was probably thinking, *How long have these guys been up here?* They scared him off and had a good laugh over it.

LEADERSHIP

"You are only as good as the people around you."
—Carol Burnett

After Port Clarence, Mark was assigned to the Coast Guard Cutter Dogwood (later replaced by the Coast Guard Cutter Kanawha) in Pine Bluff, Arkansas for five years. Mark rose in ranks from an E-3 to an E-7 in just nine years and achieved the rank of Chief. He was assigned to the Coast Guard Cutter Matinicus,

Cape May, New Jersey. At thirty years old, Mark was one of the youngest Chiefs in the Coast Guard and highly valued for his skills. But more importantly, Mark cared about his crew, and the people around him, which was critical because, as small as his crew was, they had to run and work smoothly. It is often said that you are only as good as the people around you, and Mark understood that.

> "The Chiefs that were the real mentors, leaders, honest and trustworthy guys were ones that gave me the direction that I needed. I wanted to be *that* Chief. The Chief that would not be chained to the office chair and eager to get dirty when a job needed to be done. A Chief that would allow you to make decisions on your own and stand up for you if you fell on your face. I wanted to be that Chief.
> A Chief smart enough to know when it is time to use either his position, or personal strengths to lead. Thanks to Bob, Mark Prentice, Jeff, and Tom for being *that* Chief for me."
> —Dan, retired U.S.C.G. Chief who worked under Mark for two years on the U.S.C.G. Cutter Matinicus.

A crew member once came to Mark with his head low, visibly upset because he had broken a part in engineering. Mark asked, "Well, did you break it on purpose?" Startled, the crew member said, "NO, Chief!" Mark said, "Ok, then let's go fix it, and not worry about it." The crew member flipped from downcast to motivated by Mark's pragmatic encouragement. Mark kept morale high by withholding criticism and offering assistance and direction.

Mark lives by this: "Do not be overcome by evil, but overcome evil with good." —Romans 12:21.

While Mark and his crew were busy *fostering* morale, another Captain decided to *mandate* it. The subject of military morale comes up regularly. Some say the morale of a unit is predicated on the mission accomplishment and personal recognition. Some believe it is a state of mind. I believe both, but also that it can't be forced by command mandate or things can get awkward. This next story demonstrates that:

> We were on a mundane Caribbean deployment on the 110-foot WPB operating out of Guantanamo Bay, Cuba. Our schedule had us underway for a week at a time during the thirty-plus-day deployment. After one patrol we pulled in, stopped in at the fuel pier, and then moved to our assigned berth. It was early morning and I had some time before I was able to disappear into the GTMO landscape.

I had a necessary fuel filter replacement to accomplish. If it did not happen, we could not get underway, because my fuel pressure gauges said it had to be done, period. Otherwise, a "NO-GO" as we called it.

The commanding officer (CO) held a short muster on the mess deck to tell us that the Senior Officer Present (SOPA), a.k.a. Captain of another ship, was having a party on one of the morale beaches, and we were encouraged to attend. I thought, "Well, that's nice, I hope they have fun," and I set about to do my filter change. I got the parts, my tools, and got to work. I thought it would take about a couple hours to do both engines, and then I'd go out for some fun. Well, as I am sitting on the deck plates in the middle of the engine room, I hear the forward door open. The CO pops his head in. He did not say a word, he just backed out and closed the door, and I went back to work.

About a half hour after most of the crew were gone, the Chief, Mark Prentice, comes in and asks, "Hey, whatcha doin'?" The answer was obvious, so I just looked at him puzzled. He was in civvies. He said, "The CO sent me in here to get you to go to the party at the beach." I said, "Chief, this needs to get done." He stopped me, "I know, but he's ordering you to go." "Ordering me to go on liberty?" "Yep, so don't do this and go on; just drop what you're doing and change, don't argue, they expect you to be there." ("They" meaning the CO.)

I was stunned. The CO had said that we were "encouraged to go," not *ordered*. Well, I did exactly what the Chief said. I put the tools away, moved the parts aside, showered and changed into civvies, and went to the beach party. When I talked to the Chief (Mark) during the party, his words to me were, "Don't worry about it, I got this," in his Texas drawl. So, we partied. (Mark has a way of calming a situation.)

The morning after, the boat needed to move down the pier. We needed to get underway and slide further down. I told the Chief, "The Racor's fuel filters are still wide open and empty. We cannot light off the mains." He said, "I know that" with a big smile on his face.

A little later, I was working on the filter change when the CO pops his head in, like before, and backed out. When I asked the Chief why the CO stopped by, because he never made an appearance in my engine room without a good reason, Mark's reply was, "The Old Man wanted to know why we could not move under power. I told him that he ordered you to go on liberty instead of making sure his boat could move." Mark grinned in a knowing way. I believe the CO was made quite aware that his boat did not run because of being "encouraged" to attend a command-sponsored (mandatory) morale event.

There are many stories like that in my career, but that one stands out as the most ridiculous example of one officer trying to impress another with "full crew participation" at an event. The Captain never did that sh*t again. Thanks, Mark Prentice! —Dan

ADVENTURES IN COASTING

Swimming with the Sharks. This seemed to Mark a safer experience than flying with the geriatric bush pilot, but I digress. The news article below describes an exciting scene worthy of a motion picture. Six people aboard a thirty-two-foot sport fisher boat hooked a 1000-pound tiger shark. The fishermen were participating in a shark tournament and attempted to bring the shark aboard. The weight of the people and the shark forced the stern underwater. They were sinking, and the owner issued a Mayday. Among others, Mark and his crew responded. During a harrowing rescue attempt, the shark continued to swim around them. The boat capsized, but not before Mark and his fellow Coasties ensured the safety of everyone aboard at great risk to themselves— Mark and another crew member were blown from the chopper into the ocean. (Where the shark was! Remember?)

It is worth noting that while Mark and his fellow Coastie were hanging off the boat in the shark-infested waters, the crew member who came to save them was the smallest man from the boat (usually the bigger men would do the hauling). He was winded after hauling the first sailor out of the water, and yelled to Mark, "Give me a minute, Chief!" Mark was thinking, *Sure, take your time while I swim with these sharks.* It all worked out, and no body parts were lost that day.

Shark fishermen rescued after capsize

CAPE MAY — There are many stories of the big fish that got away. But here is one about a fish that got away with a vengeance.

When the six people aboard the 32-foot sport-fisher *First Strike* hooked a 1,000-pound tiger shark in the ocean waters 48 miles east of Cape May, Sunday, June 12, they never expected it to turn into a dramatic rescue just prior to the capsizing of their boat.

Fishermen aboard the vessel hooked the huge carnivore 15 minutes prior to the conclusion of a shark tournament and, as they attempted to bring it aboard through the aft tuna door, the weight of the people and the shark all in one place apparently forced the stern under water.

Upon realizing they were rapidly taking on water without any means of stopping it, owner Bruce Nesbitt of Philadelphia broadcast a MAYDAY.

The Cape May-based Coast Guard Cutter *Matinicus*, en route from Atlantic City for a five-day patrol off Cape May, heard the call and responded. Following a 30-minute high speed run, the *Matinicus* arrived on the scene about two minutes after a Cape May Station helicopter.

The helicopter dropped a pump to the *First Strike*, but the fishermen couldn't get it started. When the Rigid Hull Inflatable Boat (RHIB) from the *Matinicus* reached the sinking vessel, another pump was brought aboard and it started to pump out the water.

All the while, there was this giant shark swimming around somewhere.

While the six people from the *First Strike* were taken aboard the RHIB, the rescue and assistance team of MKC Mark Prentice and MK2 Michael Maher boarded the sinking vessel. Then, Coast Guardsman William Luell piloted the RHIB the 50-yards back to the *Matinicus*.

As the first four victims climbed the ladder one by one to board the *Matinicus*, the *First Strike* capsized, propelling Prentice and Maher into the ocean. Prentice managed to climb aboard the overturned hull of the *First Strike* as the helicopter attempted to rescue them with a lowered basket.

But the prop-wash from the chopper knocked Prentice back into the ocean and blew both men away from the boat.

All the while, there was this giant shark swimming around somewhere. And even though it had been shot in the head three times by the *First Strike* crew, this fish was still alive and a serious threat to anyone thrashing about in the ocean.

"These guys had been chumming for six hours," said QM1 Rob Grant who was filming the rescue from the *Matinicus*. "And there could have been any number of sharks in the area."

As soon as the fishing boat capsized, though, Coxswain Luell immediately returned to the wreck with the two fishermen still aboard and they rescued his two shipmates.

Following the rescue, the *Matinicus* spent about 30 minutes trying to right the *First Strike*, but as darkness fell their efforts proved unsuccessful. All they could do was attach a light to the overturned craft and head for home.

The *Matinicus* cared for and brought the fishermen to the Coast Guard Base in Cape May, then departed and returned to her offshore patrol.

The *First Strike* started her final day's adventure with an early morning departure from Two Mile Landing for what was to have been a fun filled day of shark fishing. But on this day, the shark got the boat, fortunately, without injury to any of the people.

— By Harold Robitaille

30 | PREPARE TO BE BOARDED

Running with the Hornets. One of the duties assigned to the Coast Guard is to clear trees and brush hanging over waterways where boats must navigate. One time, Mark and a crew member were clearing an area and cutting trees. Unfortunately, Mark stumbled across a hornet's nest. The hornets engulfed Mark, stinging through his gear and under his clothes and mask, making him swell up like a balloon. He ran off to the water to get away from them. Unlike bees who lose their stinger after the first sting, the hornets kept on stinging relentlessly. It took five cans of wasp spray just to get them off the chainsaw so they could recover it. Mark was in such bad shape, and the Master Chief was so worried that he sat with him for quite some time wondering if he should call for a medivac!

HAZMAT on Land. Most people aren't aware that when a hazardous spill occurs on land (if it threatens a waterway), the Coast Guard responds. The call may originate with 911, but it quickly gets routed to the Coast Guard. On one such occasion, a disgruntled employee at a restaurant spilled a batch of used oil into a drainage ditch. The drainage ditch fed to a creek, which fed to a river, and the river eventually flowed to the ocean. When discovered, Mark was assigned to investigate. He determined the source of the spill, and the restaurant was fined—malicious pollution carries a $25 thousand maximum fine. The restaurant received the largest fine possible at that time. It was larger than any imposed on Exxon, Texaco, or Dupont! Although most oil spills do far more damage, they are deemed accidents; therefore, there is no fine. Too bad the restaurant had to pay for the crime of one malicious employee, but that was the law.

HAZMAT on Water. The Coast Guard manages the National Response Center (NRC), which maintains a National Strike Force that is specifically trained and equipped to respond to major marine pollution incidents. That's a tall order considering how small the Coast Guard is. When someone calls 911, the fire and police departments respond, but in a chemical emergency, those first responders call the NRC. This includes train wrecks or other events anywhere across the country where the run-off pollution and chemicals may enter any waterway, including any aquifer. Pollution laws were written for any waterway or tributary to a waterway. Aquifers run into creeks, rivers, lakes, and streams, as well as navigable waterways. This applies anywhere in the country. On a side note, Houston, Port Arthur, and Beaumont, Texas are known as the Golden Triangle, the Capital of Petro Chemical of the World, and unofficially, as the "Cancer Triangle."

Sometimes, the nature of a hazardous spill gets misreported, and Coast Guard responders are put at risk needlessly. One time, a pipeline ruptured next to a drainage ditch. The resulting spill was reported as gasoline. Vacuum trucks showed up to siphon it up. The CG Pollution responders advised the local fire department of danger, and to evacuate the surrounding apartment complex nearby. Five hundred people in the apartments were about to wake up and start cooking and using utilities in the presence of combustible fumes. A good call on the Coast Guard's part, but what they weren't told is that it was *not* gasoline, but unleaded gasoline which is handled differently. Coast Guard members were overexposed to the Benzine which at the least causes puffy eyes, and at worst, leads to cancer. This happened on several occasions all because the Coast Guard was misinformed of the chemical or cargo (oil, chemical) spilled.

> Mark recalls rescuing over 2,000 Cubans in his career, and there were times when some held boxes. After being rescued, they would open the box releasing a pigeon that would fly back to Cuba telling their family they had been rescued.

Two Different Worlds. One time while fighting back a hole in the fuel line on a generator, Mark put his hands over the hole and held the fuel line to keep the spray from going everywhere. His pants were soaked in diesel fuel; if the generator had sparked, he would have been dead. Finally, "Sparky," the electrician, swapped out the generator (it was an old generator). The guys outside were in fire suits and goggles. When they came in, they wanted to spray him, but he screamed, "NOOOO!" Mark did not want to get wet while the generator was still running with a charged fire hose. Water was their primary firefighting tool above deck, but a HUGE NO (below deck in engineering) with fuel and electricity. Water and electricity don't mix, as most people know.

Mother is Looking for You. While serving aboard the Coast Guard Matinicus, all hell broke loose when they were out to sea in a severe storm. It was so bad that it tore off all the antennas, taking out all electronics, lighting, and radio communications except Ultra High Frequency (UHF) radio. The crew survived the storm, but they had to make repairs, and they were unable to see anything or even radio out their position to home base for hours (under normal circumstances, they reported their status hourly). Mark felt his way through the darkness to the top deck to breathe, have a cigarette, and work the problem over in his mind. The night was dead quiet after the storm, and pitch black with no moon, stars, or ship lights to provide the slightest visibility.

As Mark lit his cigarette, a huge floodlight blinded him from above. It came out of nowhere, silently, like an alien spacecraft or a divine messenger! "It scared the sh*t out of me." Mark raced to the bridge. The UHF radio buzzed. "Matinicus! This is Magnum 44." Magnum 44 was a silent and friendly (if not initially frightening) helicopter. Magnum 44 continued, "Mother is looking for you!" "Mother" was comical slang for home base. The Captain of Matinicus conveyed the disabled status of their electronics, and the pilot of Magnum 44 farewelled them, "Magnum 44, we will report back to Mother." The Matinicus was still (temporarily) dead in the water but relieved to know that at least their whereabouts were conveyed to good ol' Mom.

On a Lighter Note—with a Flare. Mark's boat was patrolling in a designated area—over 10,000 miles of water—near the eastern side of the Gulf of Gonave, Haiti. To kill time, the crew participated in target practice with their .50 caliber machine guns, shooting and sinking empty oil drums in the water. The tracer rounds bounced off the water and up into the air (every fifth round is a tracer round). It is not normally an issue. That is, unless you are being observed by a foreign Navy.

The High Frequency (HF) international coalition was used at that time, and Mark's boat's call sign was "Mike." The radio sounded, and they received a message from "Victor," a Venezuelan warship. In a thick heavy accent (English was not his first language), Victor asked, "Uh, Mike, this is Victor. Are you shooting off (pause) flares?" Flares are acceptable; live rounds within Haiti are not! Shooting a machine gun within that boundary could be perceived as an act of aggression or war. The Coasties had not realized other ships could see them over the horizon. To de-escalate the potentially tense situation, the Officer on Deck (OD) said, "Um…yes, we're shooting flares; that's right, flares." So, the Coasties stopped shooting their "flares" and there was no international incident that day.

Death by a Thousand Pings. Mark's bunk was in the front of the boat, under the gun mount. Boats and ships are programmed with an Identification Friend or Foe number (IFF). Mark's boat was assigned an incorrect IFF number; as a result, their boat came up as the U.S.S. Enterprise which is a 2,000-foot-long ship, while Mark's boat was a mere 110-foot boat. Ships all pinged each other for identification purposes, and when Mark's 110-foot boat pinged as the U.S.S. Enterprise, the ships would re-ping for verification. A 2,000-foot ship was too big for those waters, and it did not match what they were looking at, which was Mark's 110-foot boat. This night-pinging near Mark's bunk mimicked Chinese water torture. The Navy finally identified the problem, and the IFF number was corrected. It's a funny story now, but back then the sleep deprivation was not funny.

THE RESCUERS

The Bible says, "There is no greater love than this, that a man lay down his life for his friends." (John 15:13 KJV) People don't realize that the Coast Guard loses boats all of the time—they capsize (they flip over)—and that means potential loss of life. The inlets can get so rough with fifty- to sixty-foot waves or more, but the Coasties still try to get out to rescue people. They very seldom lose people, but the few losses bring on the nightmares. Picture Mark in his tropical blues uniform, covered in blood, and a man speaks his last words: "Save me." The nurse comes with hydrogen peroxide to help get the blood out, and the doctor says Mark could not have saved him because a bullet had severed the man's aorta. It doesn't help Mark to know that he couldn't have done more. The devastation stays with him; the nightmares are real, and the memories are something he just has to live with.

In another instance, there were ten people out on a raft for eight days, and the grandmother's husband died. They tossed him over and let the sharks eat him. Mark and his crew came upon them, the sun was beating down while they were pulling the people out of the water, and they were so sunburnt that their skin just rolled off their bodies into Mark's hands. They were screaming in pain, but Mark could not let go. He had to get them out of the water before he could treat their wounds. Not everyone in the Coast Guard is an EMT (they finally started giving the Coast Guard some Navy corpsmen, but not in this instance). Mark had to tend to all their wounds that day—it sucked that he was the only EMT on board, and even worse that there was nobody else who had any medical training. To make matters worse, there were also no gloves.

> When people are lost at sea, salty water will not quench their thirst, and in fact, drinking too much of it can kill them. Sun exposure is devastating. Mark describes bodies burnt

> so badly that their noses would peel off—people who looked like something from "The Walking Dead." Things like Preparation H are a big deal; people do not realize that the insides (of your body) come outside when you are in the water too long. When you are exposed to salt water for an extended time, your anus (colon) turns inside out. It's not just about staying afloat until you are rescued.

In 1994, Mark and his crew picked up a number of Cubans in the Bahama straights. They had been at sea for so long that they were suffering from hypothermia, their minimal provisions were gone, and their water was gone, which left only seawater to drink. Their feet were raw and bleeding. Once they got their feet dried, Mark gave them his socks to keep their feet safe from the deck, which felt like sandpaper to them. Rescuing people had nothing to do with race, citizenship, or political status. They were people who needed rescuing, and the Coast Guard helps whomever they pull from the water—no one asks about their status.

Some rescues impact you deeply. After a big storm, ten people were on a raft, and a mother handed her three-year-old daughter up to Mark for safety. The child threw her arms around his neck so hard, she damned near broke his neck. It took two seamen to pry her off of Mark. That is how scared she was. The child was soaking wet and shaking so badly. After she was pried from Mark's neck, he was about to lose his composure. He wanted to be strong for his crew so he told them he had diesel smoke in his face and went to his cabin to "wash up." He escaped to his stateroom and cried like a baby. The little girl looked like his own daughter who was also three years old at the time. He had nightmares for two years after that event, but as a Chief Engineer and the Deck Safety Officer, he felt he had to lead by example and show strength first.

> The following sentiment is on a card Mark carries on his boat: "Though I have saved hundreds, no thousands, forgive me, Father, I fear and remember the ones I lost most."

Some rescues turn out to be comic relief. There was a man who called the station and reported his position and status. He was going to be ok and would get underway on the next high tide, but then his wife started screaming on the radio that her husband went overboard, and they were sinking. The Coast Guard got underway to the scene and was able to get a lift to the boat with a pump. The husband had gone to retrieve the rudder that had floated away and was walking back to the boat through water that was about three feet deep. The wife was in the cabin with a bucket and a sponge screaming that they were sinking. One of the Coasties replied, "Ma'am, there are a few things you need to know. First, you can't sink, you are aground. Second, I brought a big pump with me so even if you were sinking, I would pump it out. Third, I am here and you are not going to die, so go up there and hug your husband. Relax, and we will get you out of here in one piece."

And other rescues come dangerously close to being your own. A thirty-day deployment to Gitmo was coming to an end, and rather than risk returning home late (which would result in fines and reprimands to his permanent record), the Captain decided to risk taking the ship through a storm. The ship took a turn from the Windward Pass into the Bahama Straights. Mark's stateroom phone rang. The Senior Chief asked about using flank speed ops (full speed, fastest). Mark said, "No problem," and headed to the bridge. The sea was rough, and en route, Mark climbed the ladder to the bridge. Holding on with all his might, he fought to keep his feet on the ladder. At that moment, a great wave struck the ship from the stern (behind), lifting the rear of the ship into the air. The ladder turned horizontal, and Mark's feet flew off! Luckily, he had a vice grip on the rails that prevented the ladder from flinging him over into the communications equipment.

Had he fallen onto the equipment, he would have broken his back. He heard the Senior Chief yell, "CAN I GO FULL ASTERN ON STARBOARD MAIN?" It was the obvious move to make, and Mark thought, *Why aren't you doing that already?*

So, he screamed—with feet dangling—"YESSSSS DAMMIT!" Mark pulled himself back onto the ladder, and just as he got to the bridge, the bow (forward part of a ship) "submarined" into the water. No crew members were lost, but it was a storm to remember. The ship sustained damage and turned back to Gitmo for repairs, which of course, made them even later returning from deployment. It was unwise to risk the storm, but when people face punishment for making safe decisions, risky decisions result.

And then there are the rescues that "never happened". One night (when Mark was on the Mississippi), tow boat captains started screaming that there were sixty "civilians" in the water swimming (which is gross because, at that point in the Mississippi, the water is disgusting). Ship captains were terrified to strike swimmers in the water and were forced to choose between killing a person and running their ships aground. The situation was also backing up commercial trade traffic on the Mississippi. When the swimmers finally got out of the water, black fifteen-passenger vans with tinted windows and Virginia state license plates picked them up and drove off. The "swimmers" were dressed all in black with camo-painted faces (possibly CIA or Special Forces black ops training involved?). They did not call for permission, but they caused the shutdown of the Mississippi—a training exercise that shut down millions of dollars of commerce that day. It was never in the news.

A SEAT AT THE LONG TABLE

After twelve years, while stationed at the U.S.C.G. Station in Atlantic City, Mark's dream came true, and he attained the rank of Chief Warrant Officer (CWO). He started his career as a non-commissioned officer (E-3), made his way to Chief (E-7), and was now honored with the rank of Chief Warrant Officer (CWO). Mark was transferred to Pensacola, Florida for (fondly named) "Knife & Fork school" or "Mustang University" for non-comms that become officers.

Chief Warrant Officer, Mark J. Prentice.

After training, Mark was assigned to the U.S. Coast Guard Marine Safety Officer (MSO) Houston-Galveston in Houston, Texas. Mark was a Senior Marine Inspector, inspecting chemical ships from around the world, and as such, Mark boarded many ships from many different countries. The Mercy Ships were usually squared away and passed inspection. Doctors with lifesaving equipment made sure it was all in working order. However, Mark found safety violations on some other ships. These ships were delayed until their violations were resolved, and when that happened, Mark took heat from the upper ranks and was called to the "Long Table."

In the Coast Guard, a "Page 7" is a write-up to a service member's permanent file either for an "Atta Boy" or a "Bada Boy," and Mark was no stranger to either. He had an extremely successful career—lots of "Atta Boys"—but that also came with the occasional offense to the odd Admiral, "Big Deal," or foreign dignitary.

On one occasion, Mark's Captain received a call from Sweden. The owner of Stolt Nielsen, a Swedish billionaire, was not happy that his chemical tanker was being held at the dock for violations. Being held at the dock cost his company $1 million per day, and they wanted the ship released. Mark was called to the Long Table. *The Maritime Industry in Germany had cleared it with flying colors, so why was the U.S. holding their ship?* Well, for one thing, they had a paint locker in the bow of the ship with no explosive-proof fittings.

The locker was in front of a collision bulkhead, which is a clear violation of international safety standards (translate: unacceptable).

Paint is flammable, and it needs to be in the aft (back of the ship) in explosive-proof containers. Mark showed the Captain the Integral Code for gas ships: nothing explosive is allowed forward of a collision bulkhead. The Captain directed Mr. Stolt back to the German shipyard that had carelessly cleared the ship for inspection. That German shipyard was supposed to be the best in the world—better than Lloyds (LRS)—and they had egg on their face by an American Coast Guard Chief, a man with no college degree but who prided himself on knowing the maritime rules and regulations to a tee. That ship sat in dock for a week until its issues were fixed.

> Mark and eight other warrant officers were invited to a formal dinner by the Captain. The Captain knew they didn't have dress whites, so he thought he would play a joke on them when they showed up in tropical dress. The dinner was in a huge hall, with at least two hundred people in attendance. A porcelain toilet bowl sat on the stage that held "Grog." Grog consisted of Kahlua, vodka, and Baby Ruth candy bars, an alcoholic sweet beverage made to look like feces in an unflushed toilet; nasty looking and hilarious.

The plan was to make guests drink the Grog as punishment for minor infractions while in training. Some selected for punishment took the walk of shame up onto the stage, sipped a little, gagged, and retreated back to their seat. At one point, the Captain decided to "punish" the warrant officers for being "out of uniform," and ordered them to drink the Grog. No "walk of shame" was going to embarrass these Coasties, so they approached the toilet bowl, then drank and loved it. Mark loves all things sweet, so he poured himself seconds—they all did. Free liquor, why not? When the Captain saw that the punishment had become a reward, he pulled an about-face and declared the "fine" was over. "Get those Coasties away from the Grog."

On another ship from Mexico, life jackets were rotting and falling apart. Mark was called to the Long Table again after the Captain received a call from the Mexican Consulate saying Mark exceeded his authority by delaying that ship. Long story short, Mark knew the rules, and he won that battle. They had to buy new life jackets at a much greater expense than if they had purchased them at home in Mexico. But they had to get them before their ship could be released from the dock. Water safety and proper life jackets were (and still are) non-negotiables for a man like Mark who's pulled too many dead people from the waters.

WALK IT OFF, NANCY

The sad part about Coast Guard culture (when Mark served) was that the crew was unofficially trained to not complain or appear mentally weak in any way. Getting hurt meant putting a band-aid on it and getting back to work. There are so many injuries associated with being on these small boats, especially to new sailors. Knees get blown out easily if a sailor tries to hold down a buoy with his leg (although they are trained *not* to do that), and when a wave crashes into it, it crushes bones. Many sailors are then med-evacuated out because there is no staying on board without two good legs. But the worst part is the physical repercussions from the heat, smoke, and chemicals—sometimes they're up to their shoulders in diesel fuel and oil. It's not just hard on the outer body, it also affects breathing and hearing.

One contributing factor to health issues is the length of time spent on the boats. After a two-year tour, you are supposed to transfer to a land post so your body can heal from the toll of the boat's environment. The problem is that the Coast Guard is often too short-staffed, and valuable personnel like Mark are in high demand. He often stayed longer than the recommended time, worked with injuries, or exposed himself to hazardous materials to protect others. The Coast Guard provided relief services when possible, but that couldn't undo the damage to his body.

To assist the crew, the Coast Guard sends a Crisis Response Team (CRT) to the boat when requested, but it is usually a junior officer or Bosun. Unfortunately, they are often perceived by the crew as a stranger from admin—an outsider there to protect the Coast Guard's interests more than the men and women serving on board.

The crew also acted as firefighters using numerous cans of Aqueous Film Forming Foam (AFFF) without proper gear (a common occurrence at the time). This is now understood to be a carcinogenic material. AFFF foam is considered a forever foam, and it is now connected to prostate cancer. With all the chemicals they were exposed to, Mark once made light to his fellow shipmates that someday they would all be sitting in the Veteran's Administration's (VA's) 110 Ward, making jokes about everything they were exposed to.

Mark did not know it at the time, but Houston would be his last duty station. The chemicals he was exposed to damaged his kidneys beyond repair, and he was medically discharged in 2001 after twenty-one years of service. Despite the damage to his health and emotional trauma, Mark (like so many others) loved his job in the Coast Guard and did not want to leave it. He has no regrets about his time in service. (However, he does have complaints regarding his treatment by the VA, but more on that later.)

This quilt was gifted to Mark after his retirement, and it shows the patches from his duty stations, as well as his rank, boats, and special achievements.

Career quilt gifted to Mark.

Mark never wanted to take medical retirement, but the Coast Guard doctors had no choice; they discharged Mark and gave him five years to live. They said he'd be lucky if his kidneys lasted ten years. He was devastated and battled depression. Mark was classified as 100 percent disabled, and he was clueless about what the future held. So, what was civilian life going to look like?

At the writing of this book, it has been over twenty-three years since Mark left the Coast Guard. Doctors are counselors, at best, not God, and he is a fighter.

> "Hardships often prepare ordinary people
> for an extraordinary destiny."
> —C.S. Lewis

CHAPTER 2

MARK J. PRENTICE, LIFE AFTER THE COAST GUARD

*"Not grace to bar what is not bliss,
nor flight from all distress, but this:
The grace that orders our trouble and pain,
then in the darkness, is there to sustain."*

—John Piper

THEY WILL (NOT) TAKE CARE OF YOU

Mark was given fifteen days to get off the base after being medically discharged and officially retired. So, he was honorably discharged, but after twenty-one years of faithful service, he was only given fifteen days to vacate? What sort of transition was that? He was told to go to the Veteran's Administration (VA), that they would take care of him. Unfortunately, that couldn't have been further from the truth. Whether or not the person who said that to Mark was completely clueless or simply mistaken, the VA did not take care of Mark when he got there.

On the contrary, Mark was told by the VA, "Sorry, sir, you are not in our system. We can't help you." Mark was removed from the medical system for active duty personnel, but somehow, the Coast Guard failed to communicate to the VA to take over Mark's health care. How was that possible? Why weren't the systems connected? Mark spent the next two years fighting to get into the VA's system. Little by little, Mark learned precious information from other veterans about how to maneuver through the madness of paperwork and processes to get things done. Mark lost his job in the Coast Guard, his pay was cut (due to retirement), and his family was stressed, all while fighting kidney disease. But fight is exactly what Mark did as he started his life over again.

The good news is that the military has come a long way in providing services to their personnel over the past twenty years since Mark retired. Here is a list of websites where you can find assistance if you're a retired service member—it's a whole lot more than what Mark received:

www.militaryonesource.mil
www.linesforlife.org
www.veteranscrisisline.net
www.uscis.gov

www.psychiatry.org
www.mentalhealth.va.gov
www.girightshotline.org

Mark had been a member of his family's church for over twenty years, but for a few years after he was discharged from the CG, he was really "pissed off" at God. It was so unfair to have his job stripped from him and now to deal with the health issues *and* the nonsense from the VA! Mark has always believed in God and had faith, but the fight in him now came from anger and no one was going to tell him he was dying. After a few years, Mark softened and went back to the church he had known for years. He never gave up on God, and he figured God had heard it all. Over the next twenty years, Mark went on to become a trustee for the church. He tended to the lawns and provided maintenance. They called him "Mr. Fix-It" whenever something needed repairing.

CAN'T KEEP A GOOD MAN DOWN

Mark took a bleak situation and made the most of it. Despite being threatened with depression, he determined to make things better for himself and his family. He was going to fight for his health, survive the kidney disease, *and* continue to contribute (one way or the other) to society. Mark powered on full steam ahead, dedicating his life to volunteering: the Coast Guard

Auxiliary, Sea Scouts (Boy Scouts on water), the Texas Parks & Wildlife Department, and the Lion's Club / Leader Dogs. No one was going to bury Mark—not yet anyway. He put his much-needed skills to work.

The Coast Guard Auxiliary in Fort Cavazos, Texas received a broken jet ski as a donation. Mark decided to turn it into a training simulator. He gutted it, attached Game Boy pedals, synced them with the handrails, and then paired it with a monitor. Voila! A gamer's dream come true. It can go slow or speed up on the water, and you can crash it into the shore, ground, or other vessels—all virtually so nobody actually gets hurt. Once Mark said to a kid who constantly drove the jet ski up the bank, "I don't think you need a jet ski, I think you need a 4-wheeler the way you keep hitting the land." Much like a driving simulator, it allowed people to practice the rules of the waterways from the safety of a simulator.

*Jet ski simulator. Mark was featured in the
Temple Daily Telegram in Temple, Texas.*

Mark also started teaching Boating Safety once a month at Fort Cavazos for any soldiers and civilians interested in responsible water recreation training. He's been teaching this course now for over twenty years. So much for the "You have five years to live" part of his medical discharge, and hats off to the man who kept on fighting.

When Mark was medically retired from the Coast Guard, the doctors told him that the medication necessary for the kidney disease would most certainly cause bladder cancer. The bladder cancer came to Mark in short order, and he endured multiple bouts of chemotherapy for it.

During one of those regimens of chemotherapy, and while patrolling for the Coast Guard Auxiliary on Stillhouse Lake, Mark found himself, once again, functioning as a first responder. Mark and his crew docked at the marina and as they prepared to end the patrol for the night, out of the blue, a suspected drunk driver drove his vehicle straight into the lake next to the marina. No spectators attempted to help the driver, so Mark entered the water to check and pull the vehicle back to the shallow part of the water. Mark assisted the driver in getting out of the vehicle and helped secure the vehicle on shallow land until the tow truck arrived. The local sheriff's department responded and arrested the driver.

FOLLOWING THE GONORRHEA LADY/MANDATORY BRIEFINGS

In 2007, Mark and a colleague had been providing volunteer safety briefings at Fort Cavazos, but after a tragic accident, the safety briefings became mandatory for every soldier returning from overseas deployment or combat duty. The mandatory briefings were enacted after two Fort Cavazos soldiers, aged 22 and 29, returned from Iraq and launched a boat from Cedar Gap Park to fish on Stillhouse Hollow Lake. They were in an older, twelve-foot, flat-bottom boat that one of them had modified. They had life jackets on the boat but did not wear them. They had been out most of the day when a passing fisherman warned them of a storm coming from the north. That was the last time they were seen alive. The boat sank, and they both disappeared. Their bodies were found two days later after an extensive search.

> Mark is passionate about water safety, especially these issues: (1) Wear some sort of CG-approved life jacket and (2) Stay with the boat, even if it is capsized. You will have a better chance of being found *and* living.

Most times, safety briefings were held at a small church on base. One thing Mark noticed was that he always followed the briefing on Infectious/Sexual Disease class. He called it "following the Gonorrhea Lady" because, as they waited to get into the church, they overheard that instructor teaching on genital warts and boils. He said, "I know it is important, but why couldn't we follow the Motorcycle or Vehicle Safety briefing? And why was that class here in a church? And why wasn't a sexual disease briefing given *before* deployment, not after?" All valid questions.

Another briefing was held at Abram's Field House, which held 15,000 soldiers. The bleachers were full. There were three large-screen televisions for viewing. This was the largest briefing Mark and his colleague had given. Boating safety became a high priority. And for Mark, it was even more so for children.

STATE LIAISON OFFICER

Eventually, Mark became a State Liaison Officer, reaching out to politicians across the country and lobbying for stronger regulations to protect children on the water. People don't realize that children under a certain age have no business being on a motorized craft they can't control. There isn't the same level of protection as there is when they're strapped into car seats. A person is supposed to have two feet on the deck/floor and one butt on the jet ski. Little ones don't have either. If they are on an adult's lap (note: no one is supposed to be in front of the driver), and the jet ski hits something, the child shoots off the jet ski like a baseball off of a bat. It's devastating for a first responder to pull a dead child out of the water, to say nothing of the parents who must live with the decisions that led to their child's death. Mark is haunted by those memories, and lobbying for safer water regulations is his way of preventing parents and responders from living that nightmare in the future.

If anyone reading this feels inspired to support this type of legislation, please contact your nearest local representative.

"MR. FIX-IT"

Mark had a reputation for being able to fix just about anything. That is the reason he was able to skip boot camp when he re-enlisted. The Coast Guard shipped him directly to his first duty assignment (when command staff got wind that he had re-enlisted) and arranged for his uniforms to be shipped straight to the boat. Unfortunately, that is the reason (to his family's distress) Mark was too often called out on emergency deployments. He was the go-to guy when most engineers could not fix their boat's problems. More than one captain said they would not get underway until the "Chief" was on board.

The crew called Mark "Mr. Fix-It" as a left-handed compliment. Most of the time when they went on a SAR (Search and Rescue), Mark could fix the boats in trouble rather than having to tow them to the shore for repair. The more often Mark could fix the boats, the more often the crew was held on patrol rather than getting a trip to shore for a break. It meant extra patrols for the crew, so they weren't always thrilled with "Mr. Fix-It."

Mark has explained that, too often, wealthy people buy expensive boats with little knowledge of how to fix and maintain them, which creates problems. On one occasion, Mark was called out on a SAR, and he noticed that there were, in plain view, five pieces of equipment that could have been used to repair the boat. However, the owner had no idea what these parts were for or how to use them. In all fairness to these people, most of them aren't mechanics, and it's no different than the average person calling AAA for roadside assistance, *but* the Coast Guard is not supposed to serve the private boating community like AAA.

Mark has had to be Mr. Fix-It for more than just boats. During the past twenty years, in between volunteering and his service to others, he has continued to battle kidney disease. He's had chemotherapy about every four years since retiring. Then came bladder cancer, and Mark has endured three surgeries to remove tumors, followed by more chemo.

In addition to ongoing health issues, Mark took on caring for his disabled mother, brother, and wife. He took over his mother's finances and settled her into a nursing home when she needed total care. He continues to maintain his own house and his mother's home. His brother started having seizures and was diagnosed with Parkinson's disease. Mark became his legal guardian until he died in March 2022. Mark's late wife died of a heart attack in the following October after many years of health issues. As if kidney disease and cancer weren't enough to bear, and all during chemo treatments, he suffered these two major losses. Some things simply cannot be fixed. How could life get any worse? But he had support from his children, who took time off from work to take him to his treatments. Nothing was going to stop him from getting up every day and fighting whatever battle presented itself.

THE GOOD, THE BAD, AND THE NEXT STEP

"And the truth is that all veterans pay with their lives. Some pay all at once, while others pay over a lifetime."

—JM Storm

At the time, Mark did not know I took this picture, but I shared it with him to ask permission to include it in this book. Mark is not afraid to show the bad, ugly, and tragic side of kidney disease and cancer. His courage stands out at every obstacle.

Fighting kidney disease and bladder cancer.

That being said, he is also happy to share his determination to overcome the challenges set before him. Mr. Fix-It is always searching for ways to make things better so that he can do more for others.

Gaining strength and healing.

One way Mark is "fixing" himself is through art therapy, specifically, watercolor painting. This painting shows a Coast Guard cutter cutting through a high wave. He describes the horrific waves that were sometimes fifty feet high and how it felt like they were falling off the edge of the world. It's cathartic to put it in picture form.

So after twenty years of volunteering and taking care of others (and himself), what does today look like?

⚓

CHAPTER 3

MARK J. PRENTICE, A NEW COAST

"Never underestimate the power you have to take your life in a new direction."
—Germany Kent

COASTIE MEETS CRYPTOLOGIST, A.K.A. "SQUID"

I never thought I would find love again. At the very best, I was hoping to find "like" again and maybe spend the rest of my years with a nice companion. My late husband, Pat, was my whole world, and I was sure I would never have that connection again. God had a different plan, and by His grace, blessed me with another great man, Mark Prentice. As I mentioned before, our lives ran on parallel tracks for decades: we were both military kids who experienced world travel, we are both veterans, we were both stationed at Pensacola, Florida, and we both lived in Alaska. We both cared for our late spouses until they died. But the biggest thing we have in common is our passion for volunteering.

I met Mark in December 2022. Under normal circumstances, I would not consider dating a man who had so recently lost his wife. A person needs time to grieve and clear their head, and no one wants to be someone else's rebound. No, thanks. But Mark's children encouraged me. They shared the heartache Mark had been through the previous years caring for his late wife and conveyed to me that he was ready to find joy again. We both found great comfort in being with someone who understood what each of us had gone through. We became fast friends and took no time changing our friendship to romantic interest.

I have been volunteering since I was fourteen years old, and over the decades, I plopped myself in one shelter after another across the country. It was seasonal for me, and I didn't devote myself long-term to any one place. Mark's volunteer record makes mine look ho-hum, and it had the biggest impact on my feelings for him. A generous man who knows the value of giving back, caring for others, and paying it forward with all the blessings you can. That meant everything to me—especially in a society where people can be selfish and (especially as we get older) set in their ways. I was so impressed to see his devotion to others. And at this age! And on top of all his health issues! I knew early on Mark was perfect for me.

At sixty-two years old, Mark, a retired engineer U.S.C.G. CWO3 veteran meets Linda, a sixty-one-year-old Navy Petty Officer 3rd Class Cryptologist CTR/T veteran. We were both twenty years old when these pictures were taken.

Mark's dad was in the Army, my dad was in the Drug Enforcement Administration (DEA). I had wanted to join the Navy since the fourth grade when my family was stationed in Istanbul, Turkey, where we visited the Navy destroyer, the U.S.S. Meredith. That sealed it for me. I was joining the Navy.

Fast forward to 1982. I enlisted in the U.S. Navy. I loved my recruiter; she prepared me for the best job I could have asked for—Cryptology CTR/T—but she failed to mention it was a male-dominated field at the time. We had forty people in my class in Pensacola with only a handful of women. Most people were rolled back or failed out throughout the training—it was a tough training program, and many would not succeed. Ten of us made it through that class, and I was the only woman. Most of the men were like brothers to me. I worked hard, and except for the odd sailor who didn't think I was a "real" sailor (at the time women did not go on combatants), I did very well. But those were the rules back then, and we all had to live with it. I wasn't looking for selective equality and responded, "Do I look like your congressman? If they say go to sea, I will. Now get back to work." That usually took care of the argument, and yes, we all got back to work.

Mark and I both had an adventurous side before we met. I say "had" because we are both in our sixties now, and my grandmother was right. The brain stays put at thirty-five, but the body keeps aging, and we are slowing down a little. Anyway, Mark was in the Coast Guard saving lives, battling treacherous waters, and living an adventurous career from the Arctic to the Caribbean. I was in cryptology, at the time, which was primarily an inside desk job, so I sought adventures outside of work duties by sky diving and bungee jumping. Ziplining is on my bucket list for my sixty-fifth birthday.

The first thing I noticed when I visited Mark's home was that there was a large speaker in the garage next to his workbench and a large speaker on the back screened-in porch. All on the same station—country music loud and proud—his favorite. He told me music is everything to him when it comes to keeping his morale and spirits up. Some people drink, some people golf, others hang out at bars, but Mark? Music, golf, and painting are his ways of recharging. Being from Detroit, I am more of a Motown gal, but I have listened to more country music since I met Mark than I have in my whole life. And now, "My heart's like a truck" or "I only talk to God when I need a favor!" There is so much more to sing now than Smokey Robinson. Oh, and fun fact, I now have a cowgirl hat, black with a 2¼ inch brim just like Mark's. That's right, I was informed the brim has to be 2¼ inches.

> Mark invited me to Fort Cavazos to attend his Texas Boating Safety Class. Mark created the sign and everything else needed for the class. Everything he makes is professional grade. Mark took mini Pringles cans and made buoy props for the class, and he built a Star Wars-inspired ship (with a mini Darth Vadar doll) to teach people how to tie knots.

Mark has a passion for teaching. This is because, although he has saved thousands of lives in his Coast Guard career, teaching others water safety will help others to save lives, even if it's only their own. As the saying goes, *if you save one life, you save the world.*

Before marrying Mark, I shared one of my passions with him—my first book, *No Ordinary People*, which highlighted twenty-three different people who I considered to be great leaders. It is an uplifting book, but I wrote it during one of the worst times of my life—while caring for my late husband, Pat, who died in November of 2021 before the book's publication in March of 2022. I was listed as an Amazon #1 Best Selling Author.

My first book was by Linda Haley, and now my third book is by Linda Haley Prentice.

THE CRUSTY OLD SAILOR AND THE SQUID

After Pat died, I spent the next year on sabbatical grieving, clearing my head, and writing a second book. The second book was about my mother and my late husband, both of whom I lost to alcoholism, specifically cirrhosis of the liver. Two people I adored and lost too soon. Writing was therapeutic. I copyrighted but didn't publish the second book; it was a raw, personal project that I distribute only on request. However, I did ask Mark to read it before we got married. At the risk of scaring him off, I wanted him to know what I had been through and what he was marrying into. He said it was hard to read, and he even had to walk away from it a few times, but he did read it. I felt like the luckiest woman in the world not to scare him off.

It didn't take long (February) before Mark, said, "I don't want you to go home." When I met Mark, I was clear I did not want to get married again. I was a published author under "Haley," I had my own retirement, no debt and I was not having kids (that ship sailed ten years ago). Well, he thought about it and said, "I had a forty-one-year marriage, and I want another one." That would put me at one hundred and one. But I didn't want to go home either, so I said, "Ok, let's get started." It was that simple. Two people at this age with an incredible amount in common, parallel lives. We were married that month. No fuss, no fanfare.

One of the first things Mark said to me to convey his feelings was, "I love the sh*t outta you." I laughed so hard, I put it on a T-shirt for him. That was my romantic crusty old sailor.

Mark calls me his favorite "Squid"—a slang term for Navy personnel. He got a squid key chain at the pharmacy when he was picking up his medication. The cashier asked him who he was buying it for. A child perhaps? "Why, me," he said, "I married a squid." It's endearing when it comes from the right person.

Being older, Mark and I opted for a simple wedding service at the Justice of the Peace. Mark wore his dress blues, and I chose emerald green, which is his favorite color. My dearest friends each surprised me with a bouquet. It was a quiet but special day. Thank you, Rana and Edna, for the bouquets, jewelry, and gifts.

Our day.

We jumped the gun after our vows, and didn't wait for permission to kiss.

Our reaction when the judge said, "I didn't say y'all could kiss yet."

One of the challenges of marrying so quickly? When Mark and I met, I had fifteen months under my belt since the loss of my spouse, but Mark did not; it had been only a few months for him. Naturally, the shorter time raised concerns from Mark's friends and family. The truth was that most people didn't know Mark's personal business. He was private about his home life and didn't disclose that in the years prior to his wife's death, although completely committed to the relationship, they had been estranged. His children knew and spoke of it to me. They convinced me he was ready to be happy in a new relationship. In spite of the concerns, Mark is confident that, in time, people will embrace our marriage.

STILL SAVING LIVES

On April 27, 2023, Mark put on his dress blues and headed to the Capital in Austin to meet with Texas State Representative Dr. Brad Buckley (of District 54) to discuss water safety, specifically the exemptions (from having to take a Texas Boating Safety Course) that apply to any vessel under fifteen-horsepower or windblown vessel under fourteen feet.

Again, Mark's focus is on the safety of children. The specific concerns are for children under thirteen. People are buying recreational watercraft (paddle boards, jet skis, etc.) and taking them out into waterways traveled by commercial ships without any education whatsoever. According to federal regulations, anything that floats and can be navigated on the water is considered a vessel, so that covers a lot.

The meeting started with Mark introducing himself as the Texas State Liaison Officer for the Coast Guard Auxiliary. Mark is part of the boating safety program and recently returned from St Louis. One of the topics that came up while he was there was the exemptions to the boater education program—a concern in most states.

Paddle crafts are popular and cheap, but contribute to major casualties on public waters. Another trend is the lack of common safety practices on Personal Water Crafts (PWC), especially jet skis. Precautions taught in state safety classes warn that: "A passenger should never be seated in front of an operator. Any passenger on a PWC should be able to hold on to the person in front of them (or to the handholds) while keeping both feet firmly on the footrests. Children who are too small to do this should not ride." This is in every state course, but people don't follow it. And it is not being enforced by game wardens or water safety officers who are trained by law enforcement.

The child on the lap of a jet ski operator is like an unsecured bowling ball. Unfortunately, most authorities are only concerned about whether the child is wearing a life jacket. The life jacket will survive, but the child will not. Would you want a five-year-old child on a twelve-foot johnboat with a fifteen-horsepower motor on a Houston ship channel? In Texas, that is legal. The deaths caused by these accidents often occur at the hospital due to respiratory failure, so they are not recorded as a drowning because they are taken from the water or the pool. As a result, the statistics are skewed and don't accurately reflect the danger of unsafe water practices.

These were the Texas Parks & Wildlife stats for 2020:

Boating accidents: up 67%
Boating Injuries: up 65%
Boating deaths: up 45%

In 2023, all three increased by 40%.

Mark provided the representative with a copy of proposed regulations. The manufacturers of safety devices, working in conjunction with law enforcement, have drafted proposed regulations for state legislators because they do not want their products to cause injuries or fatalities; it's bad for business. They have too much skin in the game to allow their products to be banned.

Texas State Representative Buckley was concerned that the standards are taught, but the laws are not strong enough to enforce them. Technically, a game warden can see a child on a jet ski, and terminate the voyage for reckless behavior, but most will not because too many people have taken these citations to court to fight the judgments. With the lack of legal support, game wardens are skittish about citing violators, and who can blame them? Another issue is the language used in the various laws: "for," "shall," "should," "will," "may," etc.—all are up for interpretation! Under federal law, states can decide for themselves how to interpret each term.

> There is the ship channel from Los Angeles, California to Catalina Island. Reckless thrill-seekers paddle or surf what's known as "run with the men in black" (a.k.a. "running with sharks"). It is dangerous, illegal, and threatening to ships. Ships must stay in the channel or they can run aground. When they happen upon thirty surfers in the channel, they call the Coast Guard. The Coast Guard goes out, brings the surfers on board, gives them citations, and returns them to shore.

The meeting with the representative lasted an hour. He said he would work toward eliminating the exemptions to mandate that everyone must have a course to operate. Anyone on any vessel needs three points of body contact—two feet and an ass—on the vessel. A small child can hold on to a strap, but their feet are not on a footrest or a deck, so that's no good. They are too short. And often kids have a life jacket that is too large for them. If they are thrown overboard, the child can fall out of the jacket, making it useless. These are things Mark has seen personally when pulling people or dead bodies from the water.

National Safe Boating Week happens every year in May, and Mark asked Representative Buckley if he wanted to read the proclamation on the house floor for the State of Texas. Representative Buckley stated he would try to get it on the next docket in 2025. State representatives meet every two years, on the odd year, unless the governor calls for a special session.

All in all, hopefully, Mark has a representative to help him change the laws so we do not have five-year-olds running around in johnboats on the Houston Ship Channel.

STEERING THE BOAT

The one thing that is still difficult after all these years is maneuvering and dealing with the VA—steering the boat through the waters of red tape. Mark just got his dental work completed, but it took four years! He has had difficulty getting his medications over the years (most recently his diabetic medicine because of the demand from the weight loss community). The VA did not take Mark seriously in 2018 when he reported to his primary care at the VA that he was bleeding when he urinated, a symptom of bladder cancer. He was dismissed but advised to go to the emergency room if it occurred again. Thank God Mark did because the doctors in the ER diagnosed the cancer, and he was treated with chemo, which saved his life.

Those aren't the only waters we navigate. Mark took me out on the boat for the first time. I hadn't been on a private boat in over twenty years, so Mark thought it was a good idea to teach me how to drive it. Being a quick study, I took to it like a fish to water (*ba dump bump*) and drove it just fine under his mentoring. My confidence waivered when he asked if I wanted to moor (that means dock) the boat back on the trailer. More balls than brains, I enthusiastically said, "Yes!"

The minute Mark stepped off the boat, I panicked internally. *Wait! What did I just do? Toodling around in open waters is one thing, but MOOR THE BOAT?! Oh Hell no! I'm not qualified for that! (Warning Will Robinson! Warning Will Robinson!) Lord have mercy, the steering wheel is nothing like a car so turning it too much, turns the entire boat around. And for God's sake, crash into nothing, especially the dock to the right!* And if that wasn't bad enough, two other boats were docking at the same time (there were four lanes) with men (potentially) watching to the left! *I'll bring dishonor to my family!* (Mulan) *Ok, ok, ok stop panicking, remember his training, stare at him as he guides you in.* Miraculously, I did it! I looked like a cool cucumber, but inside I was an "I Love Lucy" hot mess: fear, panic, more fear, ok less fear, a little hope...then pure exhilaration! I trailered the boat! (In other words, I put the boat on the thing it was towed on.)

I was just as scared trailering that boat as when I went skydiving and bungee jumping. What better way to overcome fear than to throw yourself off a building with your feet tied to a rubber band or jump out of an airplane, right? I was terrified, then thrilled when I did it successfully. Eleanor Roosevelt said, "Do something every day that terrifies you." For some people, that's public speaking. For me that day, it was docking the boat without damage to life or property. Mark said I did great, and that's the confidence he instills in others. He trained me, then trusted me to it.

When all was said and done, 2023 rounded out pretty well, and 2024 is looking good so far. Happily married and Mark's health is continuing to improve. I'm happy to say that I have put fifteen pounds on him (replacing all the weight he lost from chemo), and the doctors are pleased with his progress. Pretty good for someone who was written off as dead in 2001. The dear Lord had other plans for Mark.

Mark is a devoted father, passionate volunteer, exceptional husband, loyal friend, and a cancer survivor. And one thing is for sure: I am his Squid, and he is my Coastie.

⚓

CHAPTER 4

MARK J. PRENTICE, SNAPSHOTS FROM THE COAST

A Cutterman's Poem

I've seen with my own eye
Grey ships come to harbor
When the ocean is wild
And the skies clap with thunder

Meekly they motor past
White ships with stripes
Letting go lines
Heading off in the night

The sailors look up
Not trusting their eyes
You're going out THERE?
Out there to die!

> We just smile and wave
> And steer towards the gale
> There are lives to be saved
> We vow not to fail
>
> We trust in each other
> Our all we will give
> We commit with our lives
> So others may live
>
> A Cutterman knows
> When the skies are turned black
> You have to go out
> You don't have to come back.
>
> —Mark T. Holmes, 2016

Accomplished as he is, Mark does not showcase his achievements. I, on the other hand, think his accomplishments deserve a place on the wall. So when I found a bucket on the floor in his office with all these coins, pins, and medals, I thought, *No sir, we can do better than a dusty bucket on the floor. These hard-earned accomplishments needed to be displayed.* One shadow box later, they are a favorite addition to the family room wall. There are a few medals in there from his late brother, and mine are toward the bottom.

Decades of appreciation coins, medals, and gifts.

The Presidential Volunteer Service Award from President George W. Bush.

August 4th, birthday to both the U.S. Coast Guard and Mark.

Shi**y seas, waves up to fifty feet high at times.

PORT CLARENCE, ALASKA

Welcome to the Arctic, Arctic Blue Nose initiation.

Walking snow from one place to another.

Another initiation welcoming Mark to the Arctic. Don't ask, but no one got hurt.

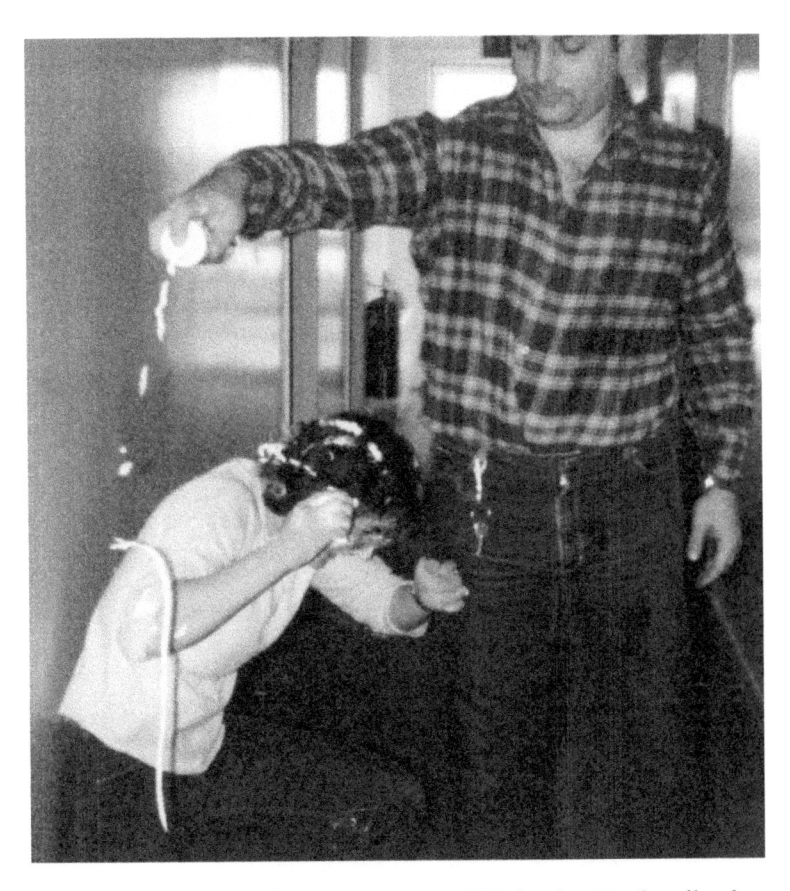

The U.S. Navy's way of initiating me into CFB Gander, Newfoundland. No one got hurt; now clean up that mess, rookie.

Canadian Forces Base (CFB), Gander, Newfoundland, Canada.

A polar bear paw print in the arctic.

Mark meets a new friend, either a young harbor seal or bearded seal.

Mark's fire exit is not so open in the arctic.

Survival training: build an igloo. If you look closely, one of the huskies urinated on it.

The 1,400-foot tower in the arctic.

Mark and a shipmate at the top of the 1,400-foot tower.

The Long Underwear Club. The one time the pilot did not get off the plane—they scared him off. Mark is the blue in the middle. The cook is on the left in a diaper; he did not have long underwear because he did not go outside. So for the picture, he adapted.

The Old Man's quarters, snow up to the roof, known as "Winter Olympics."

Off-roading in the arctic means crossing the ice.

Foil Party Hat Club to keep enemy waves from their brains.

Just me and the guys at school in Pensacola, Florida in 1982.

There were toga parties when I was stationed at CFB Gander, Newfoundland.

Good times fishing; band of brothers. Mark is second from the left.

94 | PREPARE TO BE BOARDED

Mark making friends with a local banana rat.

Please do not send me animal rights hate mail. These stories are from over thirty years ago, and they are a snapshot view of the times.

3,253 Cuban Migrants Rescued

Coast Guard cutters, small boats and Navy ships rescued a record 3,253 Cuban migrants in the waters between Cuba and the Florida Keys on 23 August 1994. This single day total exceeds the record of 3,247 Haitians who were rescued July 4.

The Coast Guard Cutter MATINICUS rescued a 47-year-old Cuban man suffering extreme dehydration at 10 a.m. A "Jayhawk" helicopter from Coast Guard Air Station Clearwater airlifted the man and flew him to a Key West Hospital.

More than 7,000 Cuban migrants have been rescued this week. The U.S. Navy guided missile cruiser USS VICKSBURG transferred 696 Cubans to Immigration and Naturalization Service officials at the Guantanamo Bay Navy Base.

More than 20 Coast Guard Cutters and several Navy ships are patrolling the Florida Straits rescuing Cuban migrants. More than 50 Coast Guard small boats are operating closer to shore and as many as 30 Coast Guard aircraft are providing air support.

Cost Guard cutters and Navy ships have rescued 11,619 Cuban migrants in August and 16,350 in 1994.

The Coast Guard Cutter Point FRANKLIN is also participating in this humanitarian mission.

Humanitarian mission.

Mark's career insignias.

Lion's Club, Leader Dogs for the Blind.

*Mark participates in Wreaths Across America (WAA).
Their mission, each December, is to remember and honor every
fallen military service member during the holiday season,
no matter what is happening in the nation or overseas.*

Fort Cavazos Safety event at Darnell Army Hospital, 2024.

After we married, I decided to take my full retirement. I had been a workaholic for decades, but with Mark's health issues (I'm his wingman now), we decided if we were going to enjoy this stage of our lives together, it was better now than later. The best thing about being retired is being able to support Mark's volunteer efforts. This picture was taken at Fort Cavazos on a weekend when the base was having an exercise, and the Coast Guard Auxiliary was invited. Three of the Auxiliary members have their own boats and can assist the base on the water as extra patrol. Me? I helped cater food for the weekend. It was a success.

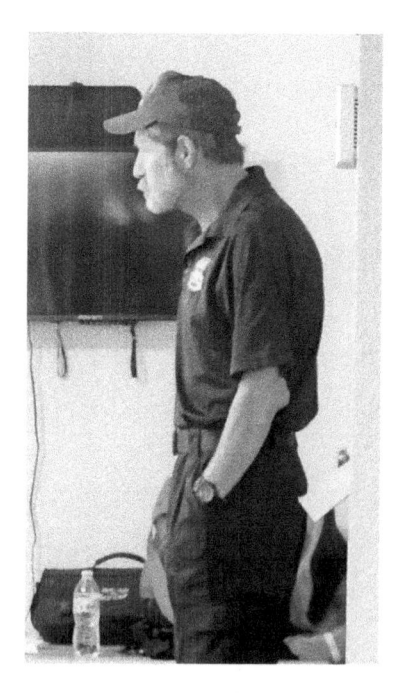

Fort Cavazos Coast Guard Auxiliary weekend.

Boating safety class.

Mark at his best, teaching water safety.

Fun swim aid, but not Coast Guard PFD Certified for children.

Mark modeling a Bum Float for adults; not Coast Guard PFD Certified. "It will only keep your drink safe."

And what kind of wife would I be if I did not take the Boating Safety Class? I refused help from the instructor, my Mark. I wanted (and received) an honest grade: 98 percent! I missed one question. Thank God, I did not "bring dishonor to my family" (Mulan). Only one error, good for me!

Mark's watercolor of a Square Rigger.

Hobby and stress relief.

CONTINUING THE FIGHT

In September of 2023, Mark and the Auxiliary were highlighted in Fort Cavazos's *The Sentinel* for their work with the Better Opportunity for Single Soldiers (BOSS) program for, boating safety classes. No one knew that the reason Mark was in civilian clothes (out of uniform) for that class was that, after the class, he was headed to the hospital for a biopsy on his liver.

We had fun with the allergy band on his wrist. It was blank, so, *allergic to what?* I helped out. I added, "Allergic to idiots." He laughed, and that's what I was hoping for. A moment of levity in the continuing battle.

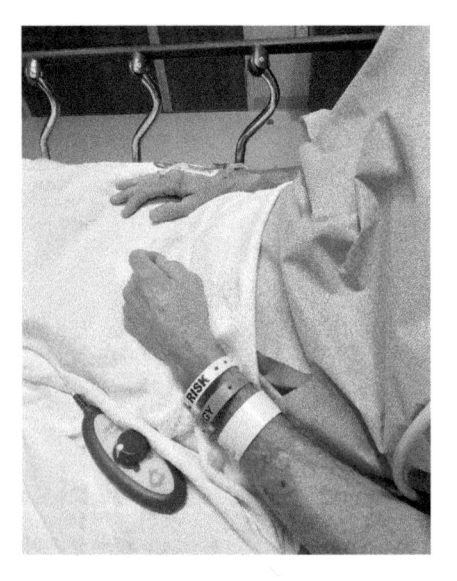

Fighting the war on kidney disease and bladder cancer.

Toward the end of 2023, and after four years as the State Liaison Officer (SLO), Mark decided it was time for a change. He wanted to spend more time with the local Auxiliary and his family. He resigned his position as the SLO. This card and appreciation coin came from the Commodore.

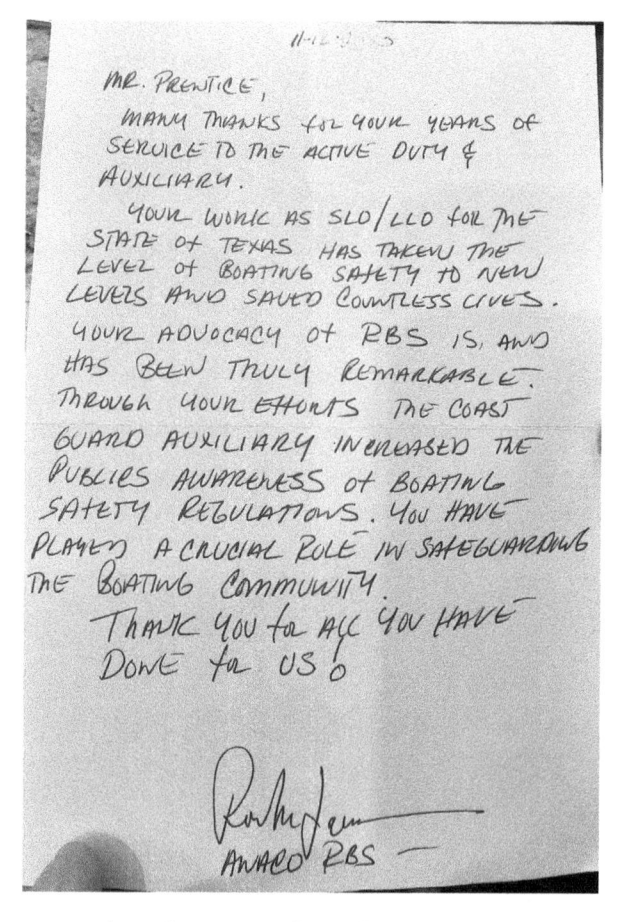

A letter from Commodore Robert M. Laurer, 2023.

Card and appreciation coin.

Mark Jr. helping his dad with the latest project.

Josh helping his dad with the lawn.

Learning to drive the boat.

Christmas Auxiliary Luncheon, 2023.

We went back to Alaska for a delayed honeymoon in 2024. We stopped by Mark's old Coast Guard station.

U.S.C.G. Ketchikan, Alaska.

ACKNOWLEDGMENTS

To **Terry**, writing a book without you is out of the question. Thank you for your invaluable editing input, friendship, and counsel. You are my hero.

To **all** who contributed; the funny, heartfelt, sad, and sometimes tragic stories were critical to giving the world a better picture of what the Coast Guard and military does for our country.

To the talented people behind the scenes:

Katie Villalobos—thank you for introducing me to Rose Friel, my Publishing Matchmaker and Consultant. You were my original Yoda from my first book, and I will never forget your care, guidance, and support. You are a rock star!

Rose Friel of Foreword Lit Consulting, LLC, my Publishing Matchmaker and Consultant. You guided me through every step effortlessly, making this an exceptional experience. I am truly grateful for you in my life.

Laura Cail, Ami Hendrickson, Olivia M. Hammerman, Lawna Oldfield and **Christian Dufner.** You all are amazingly talented in bringing my story to shine! You have a gift for bringing out the best in a writer, and it was a gift working with each and every one of you.

Milton Keynes UK
Ingram Content Group UK Ltd.
UKHW020127021224
451734UK00014B/151/J